D1262052

COPLEY

Biographies by Elizabeth Ripley

COPLEY

RODIN

BOTTICELLI

DURER

GAINSBOROUGH

PICASSO

RAPHAEL

TITIAN

WINSLOW HOMER

LEONARDO DA VINCI

MICHELANGELO

REMBRANDT

RUBENS

GOYA

VAN GOGH

VELAZQUEZ

COPLEY

A Biography

by Elizabeth Ripley

J. B. LIPPINCOTT COMPANY

Philadelphia   New York

ACKNOWLEDGMENTS

I wish to acknowledge thanks to Miss Laura C. Luckey in the Department of Paintings and to Mrs. St. John Smith, Assistant Curator of Drawings at the Boston Museum of Fine Arts, for making it possible for me to look at all the Copley paintings and drawings belonging to the museum. I also thank Miss Elizabeth Strassmann, Registrar at the Fogg Art Museum for helping me to locate and see the Copley paintings owned by Harvard University.

I express gratitude to Miss Frances Meals, Librarian at Colby Junior College, for her kindness in furnishing me a quiet and pleasant place in which to write this book.

I acknowledge thanks to the Massachusetts Historical Society for allowing me to quote from *Letters and Papers of John Singleton Copley and Henry Pelham*, 1914, and to Houghton Mifflin Company for permitting me to use quotations from *The Domestic and Artistic Life of John Singleton Copley* by Martha Babcock Amory, 1882.

I regret that I was refused permission to reproduce "The Boy with the Squirrel" in this book. The painting is on anonymous loan to the Boston Museum of Fine Arts and may be seen, on occasions, at that museum.

ILLUSTRATIONS

JOHN COPLEY was frightened when his mother asked him to tend her shop on Long Wharf. He felt small and helpless when big loudmouthed sailors, just landed in Boston after a long trip from England, reeled up to the counter demanding Widow Copley's fine tobacco.

But he always felt secure when quiet, well-dressed Mr. Pelham called asking to see his mother. Then Mrs. Copley would let him go to his room upstairs, where he spent hours drawing pictures. Shyly he showed his drawings to Mr. Pelham who told Mrs. Copley that her son had talent. If the boy would come to his workshop he would show him how drawings were engraved on metal plates so that they could be printed many times.

One day Pelham took John to the painter Smibert's studio where the boy gazed speechlessly at portraits of living people and copies of paintings by great Italian artists. How, he wondered, could they capture such brilliant colors and shimmering textures? That day John decided that he wanted to be an artist. He was delighted when his mother told him that she planned to marry Peter Pelham and that his stepfather would teach him how to draw and paint.

In 1748 Mrs. Pelham opened a tobacco shop in her husband's house on Lindall's Row, far from the rough sailors of Long Wharf. John welcomed the long hours in Peter Pelham's workshop, for he wanted to learn everything his stepfather had to teach him. He handled the engraver's tools so skillfully that he was soon able to make metal plates from Mr. Pelham's pictures.

Three years after Mrs. Copley's marriage, Peter Pelham died. Suddenly John realized that he must support his mother and his stepbrother Henry who was only two. He looked over the engravings he had made. For a boy of thirteen they were good. If he worked hard he believed he could make money on his trade, for the English who had settled in Boston were anxious to have portrait engravings to send to their relatives at home.

One of John's first portraits showed a solemn, white-wigged minister, Reverend Welsteed, who, wrote a member of his church, "fullfilled a plain and useful ministry." When the plate was finished John carefully inscribed "J.S. Copley" in the left-hand corner, hoping that the name would become well known in Boston.

THE REVEREND WILLIAM WELSTEED

Mezzotint. 1753. (13⅝″ × 9¹¹⁄₁₆″)

Yale University Art Gallery, New Haven, Conn.

Mabel Brady Garvan Collection

Mrs. Pelham continued to receive customers in her shop, while John, who was as industrious as his mother, hardly ever left his studio. When his mother told him that he looked pale and tired he took walks on Sundays, although in Copley's day walking on Sundays was against the law. When a selectman threatened punishment, John explained that he needed exercise for his health.

Copley was rewarded for his labors. Soon successful tradesmen began to order portraits of themselves. Since Smibert's death there were no good portrait painters in Boston, and Copley was determined to replace him. He was confident that he could paint a likeness of his sitter but could he portray the rich colors and textures of his clients' costumes?

One of Copley's first sitters was a little boy dressed like an English gentleman. Jonathan Mountfort, wearing a powdered wig, blue coat, yellow vest, and lace-trimmed shirt, stood solemnly holding a wreath of flowers in his hands. He wondered if the pale, serious artist who silently piled colors on his canvas would ever let him rest.

When Copley was satisfied with the figure he brushed in a rough background of trees and sky, then wrote "John S. Copley" in the lower right-hand corner of the canvas. He was pleased with the effect of shiny textures and bright colors, but he knew he had much to learn. It was easy to place one figure on a canvas, but could he compose a picture filled with many figures, like the ones he had seen in Smibert's studio? In England, he was told, portraiture was considered the lowest form of art. The great artists painted religious subjects and scenes from ancient myths. He spent hours poring over engravings of these pictures, then set to work copying some of them on canvas.

JONATHAN MOUNTFORT

c. 1753. (29¼″ × 24½″)

Courtesy of the Detroit Institute of Arts, Detroit, Mich.

John studied an engraving of the sea god Neptune riding in a horse-drawn chariot through the waves. The nude figures and horses were sharply modeled in black and white, but how could he achieve this effect in color? It was not an easy task, even for John who liked to paint in brilliant colors.

His painting showed light flesh-colored nudes and chestnut horses standing out sharply against a bright blue sky, but the firmly modeled figures looked as if they were made of wood. John realized that he must teach himself anatomy in order to make his figures look more lifelike.

He set to work copying other artists' drawings of separate arms, legs, and torsos which showed the muscles from many different angles. He labeled each muscle carefully, then wrote a description of how it worked. On one page he made an outline drawing of an antique statue. Each section of the nude Venus was measured to show the proportions of the ideal figure. On the same page he made a detailed drawing of the feet.

In this way Copley taught himself anatomy. Text and drawings were then bound together in a book which he kept with him till he died.

THE RETURN OF NEPTUNE

c. 1754. (27½″ × 44½″)

Metropolitan Museum of Art, New York

Gift of Mrs. Orme Wilson, 1959, in memory of her parents,

Mr. and Mrs. J. Nelson Borland.

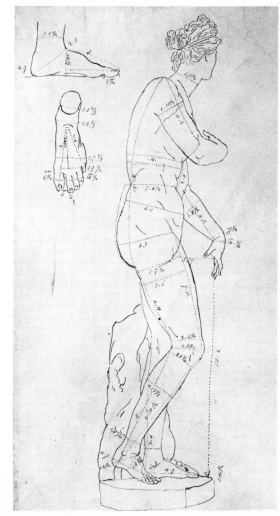

PLATE XI, Book of Anatomical Drawings (Medici Venus)

Ink drawing. 1756. (10¾″ × 17⅟₁₆″)

British Museum, London

John was worried when the painter Joseph Blackburn arrived in Boston. Although he was only seventeen, John Singleton Copley's name was just becoming known. Now he feared that his clients might prefer the fancy type of portraiture imported from England by his rival.

Copley, who was always interested in finding out how other artists worked, soon taught himself to imitate Blackburn's light graceful style. When he painted a portrait of Jane Browne he arranged the folds of her shining silk dress in sweeping curves which gave an effect of elegance to the sitter. The colors were luminous and brighter than those used by Blackburn. A ruby brooch and yellow bows added notes of rich color to her lavender silk dress. The curve of her head and shoulders was sharply outlined against a dark blue sky. Copying Blackburn's plan he painted an oval frame around his sitter.

Twenty-two-year-old Jane Browne, daughter of a minister, lived in the prosperous New Hampshire town of Portsmouth. When her portrait was finished Reverend and Mrs. Browne commissioned portraits of themselves. Copley, like Blackburn was now known outside Boston. He received repeated letters from one client urging him to come north to Halifax, but Copley refused because he had so much work in Boston. He no longer feared Blackburn's competition and had learned all that the other artist had to teach him. He soon found Blackburn's style too artificial because he was far more interested in portraying the personality of his sitter. The graceful curves of hair and drapery began to disappear from Copley's canvases. Instead he threw a bright light on his sitter's face to bring out the character of his sitter. This strong honest style appealed to practical businessmen and merchants who flocked to Copley's studio to have their portraits painted.

JANE BROWNE

1756. (30⅛″ × 25⅛″)

National Gallery of Art, Washington, D.C.

Andrew Mellon Collection, 1942

Copley barely spoke to his clients when they came to pose. In a business-like manner he would offer his sitter a chair, then watch intently to see how he arranged his legs and hands. For a long time he would gaze at his sitter with deep-set tired eyes, until the subject wondered if he would ever begin to paint. When Copley finally picked up his brush, he was able to sketch a speaking likeness of his sitter. He seldom made friends with his clients but he understood their personalities. Each was different from the other and all were interesting.

Portly James Otis, wearing a black suit, sat solidly with legs spread, against a dark brown background. One hand rested on an open book, the other on a table. A brilliant light picked out his white stockings, hands, and head. His face was slightly turned as if he were about to make an important statement. The fifty-six-year-old lawyer, described as a "rough and ready man," was an ardent patriot who later fought for America's independence. His firm legs, strong hands, and tough, energetic face tell a vivid story of this sitter.

JAMES OTIS

c. 1758. (49½″ × 39½″)

Wichita Art Museum, Wichita, Kansas

Epes Sargent was a wealthy shipowner from the seaport town of Gloucester. Unlike James Otis he scorned the patriots who wanted the American colonies to be independent. This prosperous sixty-year-old gentleman was proud of his great fortune. One hand was thrust into his pocket, and like the English gentlemen he had seen in portraits, he rested his elbow on a Roman column. The pose was elegant and relaxed. His strong face was modeled by sharp lights and shadows and the skillfully painted hand was that of a hard-working and successful man.

"Prick that hand and blood will spurt out," the painter Gilbert Stuart remarked when he saw the portrait.

Some of Copley's portraits were sent to England so that prosperous merchants could introduce themselves to their relatives. One client wrote from Scotland that his little son, on seeing his father's portrait in his grandmother's dining room, "stamped and screamed, roared and screeched, and attempted gripping the hand." Copley was delighted. "A small child," he wrote, "is free from all false notions." He himself had not been influenced by false notions for he had taught himself to paint people as they were.

"Nature has hitherto been my only instructor," Copley wrote.

EPES SARGENT

1759–61. (49⅞″ × 40″)

National Gallery of Art, Washington, D.C.

Gift of the Avalon Foundation, 1959

Copley often felt shy with his lady clients, and treated them coldly when they came to pose. Sometimes he kept them standing for six hours at a stretch, while he mixed his colors and matched them to his sitter's skin and costume. One day a lady peeked at her portrait when Copley left the room and found that after days of work the whole painting had been erased.

In spite of the long tiring hours spent in Copley's studio his lady clients were always satisfied with their portraits. The pictures showed them dressed in the latest English styles, but they did not look like pretty mannikins wearing pearls and shiny satin dresses. Each canvas portrayed the individual personality of the sitter.

Mrs. Daniel Rogers was a charming lady who had just been married to a man from Gloucester. Copley showed her against a background of sky and trees. With great care he painted the highlights and shadows of her blue satin dress, and yellow straw hat and basket. Using thin coats of paint he brushed in the soft transparent trimming at her neck and sleeves. He modeled the face in soft light and shadow which helped to capture the sitter's youthful beauty.

The ladies who saw Mrs. Rogers' portrait were eager to be painted in this elegant and graceful style. Soon Copley's appointment book was filled with the names of prosperous and important families.

MRS. DANIEL ROGERS

1762. (50″ × 40″)

Collection Mrs. Eugene Duffer

Photo Brenwasser

Copley was glad that he had trained his stepbrother to help him in his workshop. Henry Pelham, now thirteen, was able to grind colors, stretch canvases and make appointments for Copley's sitters.

Many clients ordered portraits in colored chalk which Copley could turn out more quickly than oil portraits because he didn't have to wait long hours for the paint to dry. His friend Gawen Brown commissioned a pastel portrait of his lovely wife. Mrs. Brown's blond hair, braided in one thick plait, fell over her left shoulder. Her pale blue cloak was trimmed with ermine. Pearls decorated her neck and hair. This richly dressed lady, daughter of a Boston minister, died a few months after she had posed for Copley. She was only twenty-six. A Boston newspaper praised "the beauty of her Person . . . the brilliancy of her conversation, and the sanctity of her manners." She was, the article continued, "an Honor to her Religion and an ornament to her sex."

Copley's pastel portraits were so popular that he soon ran out of crayons. In haste he wrote to the artist Liotard in Switzerland asking him to "send one sett of Crayons of the very best kind."

"You may be surprised," continued Copley, "that so remote a corner . . . as New England should have any demand for the necessary utensils for practicing the fine Arts, but I assure You Sir however feeble our efforts . . . it is not for want of inclination that they are not better, but the want of opportunity to improve ourselves. However," Copley wrote, "America . . . I fain would hope would one day become the school of fine Arts!"

MRS. GAWEN BROWN

Pastel. 1763. (17½″ × 14½″)

The Bayou Bend Collection of the Museum of Fine Arts of Houston, Houston, Texas

There was nothing soft or pretty about Mrs. Nathaniel Appleton. This strong-minded, sixty-four-year-old lady was the wife of a distinguished minister in Cambridge whose portrait Copley had painted three years before.

Reverend Appleton's yearly salary was only five-hundred dollars, but stalwart Mrs. Appleton never demanded luxuries. She wore a black lace shawl and crisp white apron over a dark green dress. A close-fitting white cap framed her round firm face.

Copley didn't feel shy with Mrs. Appleton. He understood her direct, forthright manner and showed her as she was. Her solid figure was modeled in sharp lights and darks and the stark costume contrasted with the rich red tablecloth and chair. Her pose was unaffected and her gaze unwavering. This staunch New England housewife faced life with unflinching courage.

MRS. NATHANIEL APPLETON

1763. (35⁵⁄₁₆″ × 29¹⁄₁₆″)

Harvard University, Cambridge, Mass.

Copley, in 1765, was becoming rich. His realistic portraits appealed to his practical-minded clients, but how, he wondered, did his work compare with that of European painters?

He decided to let impatient clients wait while he painted a picture to send to England. Sixteen-year-old Henry Pelham was his model. The boy sat at a table holding a pet squirrel by a chain. It was a charming portrait, but Copley feared that it might not be well received in England where portraiture was considered the lowest form of art.

"I am under some apprehension of its not being much esteemed," he wrote, when he shipped the portrait to his friend Captain Bruce in London, but begged the Captain to tell him truthfully how the painting was received.

While he waited for word from London he set to work on the unfinished portraits in his studio. One was a portrait of his friend Nathaniel Hurd. The sitter was one of Boston's most successful and prosperous silversmiths, but Copley decided to show the craftsman in his working clothes. Hurd's wig and tight-fitting coat had been discarded. He wore a black turban on his shaved head and a loose tan silk robe over a blue-green waistcoat. His capable hands were folded and resting on a table. Beside him were two books. The title of the book on heraldry was clearly labeled to show that this silversmith had engraved many coats of arms.

Copley always felt at ease with craftsmen because he could talk their language. Hurd's head was slightly tilted, his expression questioning as if he were conversing with the artist. This relaxed likeness of Nathaniel Hurd was the most informal portrait Copley ever painted.

NATHANIEL HURD

c. 1765. (30″ × 25½″)

The Cleveland Museum of Art, Cleveland, Ohio

John Huntington Collection

"I have a large room full of pictures which would engage me these twelve months," Copley wrote a friend.

Members of the wealthy Boylston family all wanted to have their portraits painted by Boston's foremost artist.

Mrs. Thomas Boylston, Sr., widow of a rich shopkeeper, sat in a yellow upholstered chair, the crisp folds of her olive-brown silk skirt spread out around her. She wore a black lace shawl about her shoulders and her intelligent face, framed by a white cap, stood out against the dark green curtain in the background. This lively lady, mother of eight children, was so pleased with the frank, truthful likeness of herself that she commissioned Copley to paint portraits of her sons.

MRS. THOMAS BOYLSTON

1766. (50⅝″ × 40¼″)

Harvard University, Cambridge, Mass.

Bequest of Ward Nicholas Boylston

Thomas Boylston, Jr. was one of the richest men in Boston, but Copley did not picture him dressed as a prosperous gentleman. Like Nathaniel Hurd he had removed his wig and coat, but Boylston's mauve turban and brown brocaded robe were made of the most expensive silk, and his white satin waistcoat was trimmed with gold. He had just been interrupted in his work. Holding a pen in his right hand, he rested his left arm on the back of his chair as he turned to greet his visitor.

That year Copley painted a portrait of Thomas's brother Nicholas wearing the same informal clothes, but when the Boylston daughters came to pose they wore formal dresses of the latest style.

Copley was so busy he barely had time to worry about the picture he had sent to England. Then, in the spring of 1766, five months after he had shipped the painting, he received news from London. Over and over he read Captain Bruce's letter, unable to believe that the Society of Artists had shown his picture and that the great painter Reynolds had praised his work.

"He says of it," wrote Bruce, "IT IS A WONDERFUL PICTURE to be sent by a young man who was never out of New England, and who had only copies to study." Reynolds observed "a little hardness in the Drawing, coldness in the shades," but, he continued, "It excelled any Portrait Mr. West ever drew."

This was high praise indeed, for the American, Benjamin West, just Copley's age, was very popular in England. He had left Philadelphia at an early age, studied in Italy and settled in London where he painted large pictures of events in ancient history. He, too, had seen Copley's "The Boy with the Squirrel" and decided to write the artist a letter of advice.

The picture was "too liney," wrote West, the outlines too sharp, but these things could be corrected, and he urged Copley to paint another canvas to send to England.

In spite of West's criticism, Copley was elected a member of the Society of Artists, an honor never before given to a painter living in America. Encouraged by this news he set to work painting another picture to send to London.

THOMAS BOYLSTON, JR.

c. 1767. (50″ × 40³⁄₁₆″)

Harvard University, Cambridge, Mass.

Bequest of Ward Nicholas Boylston

Copley's model, a very plain young girl, knelt beside the same yellow chair in which Mrs. Boylston had sat some months before. Her black and white hunting dog stood beside her, looking at the pet bird perched on the ribbon the girl was holding. Remembering West's criticism, Copley softened the outlines so that the figure did not stand out sharply from the background. With this improvement he was sure that his painting should be well received.

Again Copley waited five months before news came from London. The report was disappointing.

"You have been universally condemned in the choice of your subject which is (of) so disagreable a character," wrote Captain Bruce. West reported that Reynolds "was not so much Pleased with it as he was with the first Picture." The drawing was correct, he continued, but "the Gown too bright for the flesh . . . the dog and carpet too conspicuous." But it was difficult to explain all these things in writing.

"I hope I have the Pleasure of seeing you in Europe," continued West, for only by seeing the great "Productions of Art" could Copley learn how to improve his work, and "if you should come to London," West concluded, "my house is at your service."

Copley debated a long time before he sent his answer. Should he give up his Boston business and settle in London where he might not be successful?

"I cannot think of purchasing fame at so dear a rate," wrote Copley. "I should be glad to go to Europe," but only if West would guarantee "a good prospect" for his future.

"Painters cannot live on art only," Copley wrote to Bruce, "tho' I could hardly live without it."

YOUNG LADY WITH A BIRD AND DOG (Mary Warner?)
1767. (48⅛″ × 40″)

The Toledo Museum of Art, Toledo, Ohio

Gift of Florence Scott Libbey, 1950

Copley stayed on in Boston where he had been well rewarded for his work. He was glad that he could give his hard-working mother all the luxuries she deserved, and now he looked forward to the day when he could afford to marry.

"I find miracles have not ceased," he wrote a friend, soon after he met pretty Susanna Clarke at the home of one of his wealthy clients. He had been flattered that this attractive daughter of a prosperous tea merchant was interested in his painting, but would Susanna's father approve of a man who had spent his boyhood on Long Wharf? Although Copley was a successful painter who wore a powdered wig and velvet suit, and although he had learned to speak the language of a gentleman, he knew that painting was regarded as a trade, not "one of the noble arts," he wrote to West. Many of his friends were simple craftsmen whose manners might shock Susanna's father.

In the fall of 1769, Copley decided to ask Susanna Clarke to be his wife, and on Thanksgiving Day "Sukey" and John were married. Copley, now a member of one of Boston's most important families, decided to move from the commercial center of the city. He bought a large farm on Beacon Hill overlooking Boston Harbor, and here he settled with his bride, his mother, and his stepbrother Henry Pelham.

Copley continued to paint portraits of his fellow craftsmen, one of whom was stocky, outspoken Paul Revere. This silversmith, shoer of horses, and maker of false teeth, was also an ardent patriot who believed that the American colonies were unjustly taxed by Britain. He protested violently against the high tax on tea which was imported from England by Susanna's father.

Copley's portrait of Revere showed him holding a teapot he had designed for some Boston merchant. Dressed in his shirtsleeves, his hair un-powdered, he sat at his work table wondering how he would decorate the piece of silver he had just completed. His right hand supported his round head, and his left hand held the round silver pot. His engraver's tools spread out before him were reflected in the polished table-top, and his skilled craftsman's fingers were mirrored in the shiny teapot.

PAUL REVERE

1768–70. (*53″ × 28½″*)

Museum of Fine Arts, Boston, Mass.

Gift of the Revere Family

Copley seldom discussed politics with his sitters.

"Political contests" are neither "pleasing to an artist or advantageous to art," he wrote to West. But Boston in 1770 was seething with political disagreement. Some of Copley's clients were Tories, loyal to the mother country, while others were Whigs who believed that the American colonies should be independent. While patriots like Samuel Adams shouted that Americans were the slaves of England, Tories like Richard Clarke believed that England and America should stay together.

"Independent we are and independent we will be," thundered Samuel Adams in the House of Representatives. He railed against the high taxes and the British governor who imported English soldiers to keep the peace. He fanned people's hatred of these Redcoats until one day sixty angry patriots hurled stones at ten British soldiers who were drilling in the public square. One soldier fired on the mob killing three and wounding eight. Adams called the event a massacre. The following day he confronted Governor Hutchinson in the House of Representatives and demanded that he withdraw the British troops.

"I saw his knees tremble," said Adams later, "I saw his face grow pale (and I enjoyed the sight)."

This was the Samuel Adams Copley painted, fierce and inflexible as he pointed to the Massachusetts Charter. Copley admired this fearless patriot who gave the American people courage to demand their freedom, but he hoped that violence could be avoided. From his house on Beacon Hill he watched "The Sons of Liberty" drilling on the Common and feared that these patriots might decide to fight. If war broke out, should he follow West's advice and move to London?

Copley debated. Business was still good in Boston and he hated to leave his farm and his mother who was too frail to travel. Then in the spring of 1771 he received a letter from Captain Kemble in New York enclosing a list of clients who wanted to have their portraits painted. The offer was too good to miss, for New Yorkers paid good prices. Once again Copley decided against a trip to England.

SAMUEL ADAMS

1770–72. (50″ × 40¼″)

On deposit at Museum of Fine Arts, Boston, Mass.

Courtesy, City of Boston

"We are fixed in a very commodious house," wrote Copley to Henry Pelham from New York.

"The city has more grand buildings than Boston, the streets much cleaner . . . but it is not Boston in my opinion yet."

"I am visited by vast numbers of people of the first rank," continued Copley. The first sitter on his list was beautiful Mrs. Gage, wife of a British general. A strong light played on her handsome face and picked out the highlights of her satin dress. Copley used the same bright light to bring out the personality of his other sitters. It played on the face of Reverend Ogilvie as the distinguished minister of Trinity Church, who preached in Dutch and English, sat at his desk turning the pages of his book. The red curtain behind him was pulled aside to show the important volumes in his study.

"I have done my best paintings here," Copley wrote to Henry, then gave detailed instructions about the remodeling of his Boston house. The studio must be nine feet high, Sukey wanted windows in the kitchen, and his mother must be given the stove she asked for. He warned Henry not to spend too much money, then asked him to add a piazza like those on New York houses.

When Copley and Sukey returned to Boston six months later, their remodeled house was ready. It was there that their first son, John, was born. Their daughter, Elizabeth, was two years older.

The Copleys lived comfortably in their house on Beacon Hill, but John often worried that he might not be able to support his growing family. Boston merchants were unable to afford expensive full-length portraits because Americans refused to buy their British goods. Copley's father-in-law was threatened by a mob because he refused to return a shipload of tea to England. In vain Copley tried to reason with the patriots. "The Sons of Liberty" were aroused. One night, in the fall of 1773, Samuel Adams and his followers, dressed as Indians, boarded Clarke's ship and dumped the tea into the Boston Harbor. The patriots were in command.

Copley soon realized that if he expected to make a living on his painting he would have to seek his fortune in the mother country. In June, 1774, he sailed for London, leaving his family in charge of Henry Pelham.

MRS. THOMAS GAGE
1771. (50″ × 40″)
Lord Gage Collection, Firle Place, England

REVEREND JOHN OGILVIE
1771. (50″ × 40″)
Trinity Church, New York

Copley wrote Sukey as soon as he arrived in England. It was good to be on land after twenty-nine days at sea. He was anxious for news of home and hoped that he and his family would be united soon.

He wrote Henry about Mr. West's warm reception. The American artists had called on Reynolds and had visited the Royal Academy "where students had a naked model." At the Queen's Gallery he saw paintings by Italian masters and decided that the problem of composing figures was not as terrifying as he had supposed. Although he had already received commissions for portraits, he was advised by West to go to Italy before he settled down in London.

In August, Copley set off for Rome to study the works of Italian artists. Sukey need not worry, because his traveling companion, Carter, spoke foreign languages. He wrote enthusiastically about his trip through France. The Paris buildings were imposing, the linen clean, and bread good. He was impressed by the green fertile country and the massive snow-capped Alps, but after two months of travel the artists were eager to reach Italy. Carter was like a slimey snail,wrote Copley, and Carter complained about his "pock-marked companion" who carried a big cane and lectured about the virtues of America.

In October, Copley wrote Sukey that he had arrived in Rome and had just received her letter with alarming news from home.

"Boston will soon be a place of Bloodshed," he wrote and urged Sukey to bring the children to London.

"The trouble you must be in will quicken my return to England," he continued, then assured her that his trip to Italy had not been in vain.

"I feel more confidence in what I do myself," he wrote. He was painting a religious picture filled with many figures which he described in detail to Henry Pelham. Like Raphael he had made "kind of a ground plan" for the composition. Then after making careful drawings of each figure he arranged them together in a final drawing. This was the drawing of "The Ascension" which Copley ruled off in squares and transferred to a canvas after he returned to England.

THE ASCENSION

1775. (32″ × 29″)

Courtesy, Museum of Fine Arts, Boston, Mass.

Bequest of Susan Greene Dexter in memory of Charles and Martha Babcock Amory

When it grew too cold to paint, Copley joined friends who were on their way to Naples. He basked in the southern sun which made oranges as big as American apples, and marveled at the ruins in Pompeii, but he worried constantly about Sukey and the children. Perhaps they had already left for England, but was his "dear mother" able to make the trip? He was anxious to head north in order to reach London before his family.

His friends, the Izards, listened sympathetically and offered to take him in their private coach to Rome. In gratitude Copley painted a portrait of his friends. Once more he tried his hand at composition by surrounding his sitters with antique works of art. Into one canvas he crowded a Greek vase, classic column, Roman statue, and a glimpse of the Colosseum. His sitters, placed at the bottom of the canvas, seemed less important than the carved gilded furniture, red brocaded curtain, and the works of art around them, but Copley was delighted with the composition.

"It will support its merit in any company whatever," he wrote Henry. Now he could settle in London confident that he could compete with English artists.

In June, he set off for Parma where he was commissioned to make copies of some Italian paintings. He found it hard to concentrate on the work because the news from home was bad.

"What I greatly feared has at last taken place, the war has begun ... The reflection is too much for me to bear," he wrote Sukey. A few days later he received good news from England. Sukey and her three children were safe in London. Her baby son, too weak to travel, was in Boston with Henry and his mother. Copley hurried to finish his work in Parma, so that he could start on his long trip to England.

"I have now travelled in 16 days 800 miles," Copley wrote from Germany. "The roads are heavy and wet," but he was glad to visit countries he had never seen.

In October, 1775, Copley arrived in London. After sixteen anxious months he was united with his family and ready to start a new life in England.

MR. AND MRS. RALPH IZARD

1775. (6'9" × 88½")

Courtesy, Museum of Fine Arts, Boston, Mass.

Edgar Ingersoll Browne Fund

While Sukey and the children visited friends from Boston, Copley hunted for a house in London. Soon the Copleys and Sukey's father were comfortably settled in a house on fashionable Leicester Square. Almost every evening they were entertained by American friends who, like themselves, were refugees from the war. Many of these were Tories who were opposed to American independence. Copley, not wishing to take sides in politics gradually withdrew from social life, but he was happy spending his evenings with his family and his days working in his studio.

He was confident that he could make a living on his portraits, but commissions came in slowly. His American friends who had lost their property in the colonies could not afford portraits and Copley began to wonder if he should paint historical pictures which had made West popular in England. He decided he would try his hand at scenes from ancient history as soon as he received the casts of antique statues he had bought in Rome. The casts arrived at last, smashed beyond repair. In vain Sukey tried to comfort him. Copley was depressed. He missed Boston and worried because his farm was occupied by British troops. Unlike his Tory friends he believed that America would win the war, but, he wrote,

"The country which was once the happiest on the globe will be deluged with blood for many years to come."

While Copley waited for commissions he painted a portrait of himself. Wearing a white wig and red coat he studied himself in the mirror. His traveling companion Carter had been right, that "His small eyes, after fatigue seemed a day's march in his head." But Copley did not hesitate to show himself as truthfully as he had shown his sitters. With the confidence of an expert portrait painter he quickly brushed in an honest likeness of himself.

SELF PORTRAIT

1776–80. (18⅛″ diameter)

Private Collection

"In passing through Leicester-square, I called in at Mr. Copley's," wrote a friend of Richard Clarke's. "He was then at work on a family piece containing himself, Mr. Clarke, his wife and four children, of all of whom I observed a very striking likeness."

Copley had placed himself in the background. Because of his American accent and plain manner he often felt inferior to his Tory friends, but he was proud of his distinguished father-in-law and charming wife and children. Mr. Clarke sat in the foreground holding Susanna Copley on his lap. This was his youngest grandchild who had been born in England. Sukey sitting on a sofa bent tenderly toward her adored son John, who wound one arm around his mother's neck. Three-year-old Mary leaned across Sukey's lap and Elizabeth, Copley's oldest and favorite daughter, stood independently in the center of the picture. Trees and a classic column framed a distant landscape as they had in Copley's portrait of the Izards. Leaning against a fold of the curtain on the left was a child's doll and Sukey's feather fan.

When Copley showed the family portrait at the Royal Academy in the spring of 1777, a critic wrote that the still-life details were so "glaring" that the effect of the figures was destroyed; but many were attracted by the happy family scene. Sir William Pepperell who had known Copley in America commissioned a group portrait of his family which was shown at the Academy the next year. Once again critics were indifferent, but Copley did not go unnoticed. Every day visitors to the Academy crowded around another Copley painting which one writer called "one of the most striking pictures in the Great Room."

THE COPLEY FAMILY

1776–77. (72½" × 90⅜")

National Gallery of Art, Washington, D.C.

Andrew Mellon Fund, 1961

Visitors to the Academy stood spellbound in front of Copley's picture, wondering if the young man floundering in the bloody water would be eaten by the shark. Would the harpoonist in the boat spear the attacker before it was too late, or would the boy's companions pull him from the water before the shark's jaws snapped together?

Copley knew the answer for he had heard Brook Watson tell the story many times. During the long crossing from America, Copley used to listen fascinated as the wealthy merchant, stumping about the deck on his wooden leg, acted out the scene.

Twenty years before, young Watson was swimming in the Havana Harbor. Suddenly a shark flashed through the water striking Watson in the leg. The second strike snapped off his foot. Then just as the shark was about to strike again the boy's companions pulled him from the water.

Brook Watson was pleased that his gruesome story made a deep impression on the quiet American artist. Soon after Copley arrived in London the eccentric merchant commissioned a picture of the scene. It was a startling subject, unlike any event portrayed by other artists, but Copley seized this chance to show that he could paint events as well as portraits.

He studied maps and engravings of the Havana Harbor so that he could portray a realistic setting for the scene. Morro Castle on the right and the Cathedral tower on the left could be easily recognized by people who had been in Cuba. He made many sketches until he was satisfied that the composition expressed the tense excitement of the moment. He drew studies of each figure until he found the poses which portrayed anxiety and horror. Then he ruled off the final drawing in squares and enlarged it on a canvas.

The dramatic light and dynamic composition made a deep impression on everyone who looked at Copley's picture.

"I cannot take my eyes off that painting," one of Copley's servants said.

Even the newspapers were enthusiastic.

"We congratulate our countryman," one critic wrote, "on a Genius, who bids fair to rival the great Masters."

WATSON AND THE SHARK

1778. (71¾″ × 90½″)

National Gallery of Art, Washington, D.C.

Ferdinand Lammot Belin Fund

Copley's mother wrote from Boston urging her son not to work too hard.

"I raise a thousand fears concerning your . . . close application to your art," she wrote and cautioned him to take his daily exercise.

In spite of his mother's advice Copley spent every daylight hour working on the biggest canvas he had ever painted. Encouraged by his success with "Watson and the Shark," he was confident that he could portray a more important subject.

No event in recent history had attracted more attention than the death of the Earl of Chatham. Chatham was popular in America because he had fought to give the colonies their rights and admired in England because he did not want Britain to lose her colonies. When Britain faced defeat in the War of Independence, Chatham, old and gouty, hobbled into the House of Lords to deliver an impassioned speech. Leaning on his crutches he urged that Britain make every effort to hold America. Suddenly he grasped his chest and fell backwards in a faint. Horrified Lords rushed to help him. Only his bitter opponent Lord Mansfield sat unmoved. One month later Chatham died.

Copley spent months making sketches of the scene. When he was satisfied with the composition he painted fifty-five separate portraits of each Lord. Lord Mansfield was the only nobleman who refused to pose because Copley had placed him in the background.

In the spring of 1781, Copley showed "The Death of the Earl of Chatham" in a special hall. Twenty thousand people paid admission to see the picture they had heard so much about. Many spoke in whispers "as if at the bedside of a sick person," wrote one critic. A strong light played on Chatham's reclining figure and on the faces of the Lords around him. Another ray picked out Lord Mansfield sitting among his supporters. Flickering light illumined the Lord's red robes, making dramatic accents through the picture.

Visitors pored over the catalogue which identified each Lord's portrait.

"The resemblances are considered perfect," a reviewer wrote. For the first time Copley had used his talent as a portrait painter to portray an event in history.

"This is the most arduous work of any kind," wrote Copley, "hitherto undertaken in any . . . country."

THE DEATH OF THE EARL OF CHATHAM

1779–81. (90″ × 121″)

Reproduced by courtesy of the Trustees of the Tate Gallery, London

"The Death of the Earl of Chatham" attracted more people than the Royal Academy show that spring. Academy members grumbled that because of Copley their receipts were low. They were pleased when some writers criticized "The Death of Chatham." It was obvious, one critic wrote, that Copley had never been inside the House of Lords. The room was incorrectly drawn and "Mr. Copley ought to know that their Lordships are never robed when in debate." Copley, who had purposely shown the Lords in scarlet robes in order to make the picture more dramatic, paid little attention to his critics.

Copley at forty-three was rich and famous. He had made twenty-five thousand dollars on the private showing and looked forward to making more from the sale of engravings of the picture. He did not know that the engraver would take so long to make the plate that angry subscribers would demand their money back. Nor did he know that he would never sell the painting.

Sukey was delighted that her husband's triumph brought him many clients. When expensive carriages drove to their door she knew that some important person had come to have his portrait painted. Even Lord Mansfield, who had refused to pose, sat to Copley two years later. Dressed in a scarlet robe trimmed with ermine he sat at his desk. His face framed by a white wig was far more genial than the stern impassive profile Copley had pictured in "The Death of Chatham."

Copley's studio was becoming overcrowded, with no room to show his finished pictures. In 1783, soon after their baby Jonathan was born, the Copleys and Richard Clarke moved into a house on George Street in a quiet part of London. Copley hung his finished pictures in the central skylighted room. The small room behind this lofty gallery became his studio. Here John Singleton Copley received many important clients.

EARL OF MANSFIELD

1783. (88″ × 57½″)

National Portrait Gallery, London

Elizabeth often tiptoed into her father's studio to watch him paint. She was now thirteen, old enough to talk intelligently about his pictures, but she never disturbed him while he worked. When Copley had portraits to paint outside London he often took his favorite daughter with him. She was proud that her father had so many important clients and impressed that he could paint such perfect likenesses of his sitters. How skillfully he had captured the self-assurance of Midshipman Augustus Brine. This striking portrait showed a handsome youth, just Elizabeth's age, dressed in the uniform of the British fleet. Glittering gold buttons decorated his white vest and the edge of his blue jacket. His gold hair hung loosely about his neck. This arrogant young man, who later became an admiral, grasped his hat in one hand, the other rested on his hip. In an opening on the right a ship could be seen tossing on a stormy sea.

There was little conversation in Copley's studio, but when Americans came to pose they were asked about the war. Each year the news was more encouraging. Under the leadership of General Washington the Americans were winning many battles. Then in October, 1782, news came that Lord Cornwallis had surrendered. The long agonizing war was over. An elated Copley joined the crowds which poured into the House of Lords to hear King George acknowledge American independence. As he was leaving he met one of his American clients whose portrait had just been completed. Elkanah Watson was surprised when Copley asked him to come to his studio while he put the finishing touches on the picture. He watched with interest as Copley placed the portrait on his easel. It showed the prosperous merchant standing beside a table covered with official documents. Through an opening in the background one of his merchant ships could be seen on the horizon. Without a word Copley placed dabs of red, white, and blue on his palette, then with a fine brush painted the stars and stripes flying triumphantly from the mast.

MIDSHIPMAN AUGUSTUS BRINE

1782. (50″ × 40″)

The Metropolitan Museum of Art, New York

Bequest of Richard De Wolfe Brixey, 1943

Americans received a warm welcome at the Copley house on George Street. One of these was a fellow Bostonian, John Adams, who had come to arrange a peace with England. This brilliant lawyer, three years older than Copley, had worked tirelessly for his country's independence. He was a practical man who cared little about art.

"A luxury tool of the upper classes," he once said, but when he visited Copley's studio he almost believed that the portraits were alive.

"You can scarcely help discoursing with them," he wrote.

Copley was pleased when Adams commissioned a portrait of himself, although the stocky ambassador with a big head was not a handsome subject. Adams soon found the hours of posing tiresome and wrote his son that he hoped that this "Piece of Vanity" would be the last.

When the portrait was finished Mrs. Adams visited Copley's studio and was delighted to see that the picture showed her husband dressed in his best brown velvet suit, with a sword hanging by his side. It had not been easy for Adams to dress like an ambassador when his budget was so small. This sensitive man, who had often been snubbed in London, looked imposing. In one hand he held a scroll. His other hand pointed to a globe, as if he believed that he had the world before him. Set in the opening above the globe was a statue of a Roman goddess holding the olive branch of peace.

Mrs. Adams was enthusiastic. It is "a very good likeness," she declared, and "a most beautiful picture."

JOHN ADAMS

1783. (*93¾″ × 58″*)

Harvard University, Cambridge, Mass.

Bequest of Ward Nicholas Boylston

The publisher John Boydell was quick to see that Copley's historical paintings would bring in money. Soon after he saw "The Death of the Earl of Chatham" he commissioned Copley to paint another history painting from which engravings would be made.

No recent event had stirred the British more than the death of Major Peirson. Few men were more admired than this brave young officer who, one winter night, turned back the French invaders from the Isle of Jersey. After a fierce battle the French retreated, but as they fled one of their bullets killed the British leader. Everyone who had read about the tragedy was eager to see it pictured on a canvas. Copley could not have chosen a more popular subject for a painting.

The picture would show a scene of violent action, in which scarlet uniforms, flying flags, and flashing steel would be lighted by clouds of gun smoke; but he knew that there would be months of planning before he could paint the event on canvas.

Elizabeth often wondered if her father would ever start to paint. He studied drawings of the town where Peirson had been shot and talked with the soldiers who had been with the major when he died. He sketched a group of soldiers carrying Peirson's body, with the name of each written above his hat. Then he transferred these figures to a canvas, drew a dead soldier in the foreground and pursuing soldiers in the background. The composition was complete except for the civilians who were trying to escape. Copley picked up his brush and quickly outlined a fleeing family on the right.

One by one Copley painted portraits of each soldier, then made more sketches of the fleeing family. With each drawing the composition changed. Instead of a father he showed a mother with a baby in her arms, then added a little boy with arm upraised running beside her. Sukey and the Copley nurse stood patiently holding Jonathan in their arms, but young John Copley wearing a broad-brimmed hat squirmed when he had to be his father's model.

For two years Elizabeth waited to see the finished painting. Finally, in the spring of 1784, "The Death of Major Peirson" was ready to be shown.

Study for the DEATH OF MAJOR PEIRSON
Chalk drawing. 1782–83. (14″ × 22⅝″)
Reproduced by courtesy of the Trustees of the Tate Gallery, London

DEATH OF MAJOR PEIRSON
Oil sketch. 1782–83. (27¼″ × 35¼″)
Yale University Art Gallery, New Haven, Conn.
The John Hill Morgan Collection

Studies for the DEATH OF MAJOR PEIRSON
Drawing. 1783. (13⅞″ × 22½″)
Courtesy, Museum of Fine Arts, Boston, Mass.
M. and M. Karolik Collection

Elizabeth was impressed when King George asked for a private showing of "The Death of Major Peirson." The day before the exhibit opened Copley sent the painting to Buckingham Palace, then waited anxiously for the king's opinion.

For three hours King George studied the picture he had waited so long to see, then "expressed himself in the highest terms of approbation," wrote a reporter in *The Morning Herald*. He praised the spirited composition, brilliant colors, and dramatic contrasts of light and dark. Again and again his eyes returned to the central group holding the major's body and to the striking figure of the Negro servant firing on the soldiers who had killed his master. The queen brought the little princesses to see the painting. They too were enthusiastic.

The next day the exhibition opened. From eight in the morning till midnight the room was filled with milling crowds of people who paid a shilling to see the picture the king had praised. They were not disappointed. It was far more brilliant and exciting than any battle picture they had seen. Each visitor received a pamphlet which included a key to the soldiers portraits. Some visitors recognized the fleeing family on the right. The handsome blond-haired boy was young John Copley, the woman with the baby in her arms was the Copley nurse, and the lovely lady with upraised arms was the artist's wife.

Once again Royal Academy members watched alarmed as people flocked to Copley's private showing. As Copley grew richer the Academy receipts declined, but he showed little concern for the opinion of his fellow artists. After years of hard work he had at last been recognized as England's best historical painter, he was flooded with orders for engravings, and, before the exhibit closed the king gave him permission to paint a portrait of his three youngest daughters.

DEATH OF MAJOR PEIRSON

1782–84. (97″ × 144″)

Reproduced by courtesy of the Trustees of the Tate Gallery, London

Princess Amelia cried when her nurses tied the bow of a huge frilly hat under her chin and sat her in a carriage. Princess Sophia tried to comfort her, but she too was miserable sitting crosslegged behind her sister; and the oldest princess, Mary, was sure she would faint if she had to hold her arm up one minute longer.

Copley, painting silently, never noticed that the princesses were unhappy. In vain the nurses begged the queen to speak to Mr. Copley. Queen Charlotte refused to interfere. Day after day the unhappy princesses were brought to the painting room until the picture was completed.

In 1785, Copley sent "The Three Youngest Daughters" to the Academy. It was the gayest picture he had ever painted. Princess Mary, holding a tambourine, was pulling her sisters in a carriage, while three spaniels leapt and barked about her. She wore a white and yellow dress with a lavender sash about her waist. Sophia's dress was pink and her broad-brimmed hat and sash were blue. Amelia was dressed in white except for a blue sash tied in a big bow around her waist. Bright colored flowers, birds and fruits made a gay border around the merry trio.

Copley was not prepared for the reception his gay picture would receive. Many artists who were still bitter about Copley's private showing were quick to condemn his only contribution to the show.

"A Bedlam of Still Lifes," one critic called the picture. Had Mr. Copley concluded that "fine feathers make fine princesses"?

"All flutter and folly, flowers and ribbands," wrote another critic. The jealous artists had been avenged and Copley never received another commission from the king.

That same year disaster struck the house on George Street. The two youngest Copley children fell gravely ill. Copley and Sukey watched helplessly at their children's bedsides, unable to relieve the agonizing sore throats which slowly choked them. In October, Susanna and Jonathan Copley died. Sukey was stricken by the loss, while Copley could only forget his grief when he was working in his studio.

THE THREE YOUNGEST DAUGHTERS OF GEORGE III
(Mary, Sophia, Amelia)

1785. (104½″ × 73″)

Visitors to Copley's studio found him standing on a platform working on an enormous canvas.

"The picture was immense," (18 × 25 feet) one reporter wrote, and wound up on a roller "so that any portion of it at any time might be easily seen."

For two years Copley had been working on this battle scene commissioned by the London City Council. It was not an easy task to tell the story of the relief of Gibraltar on one canvas. Copley had read many accounts of this recent English victory when the British set fire to besieging Spanish ships, while General Eliott and his officers directed the operations from the Rock.

Copley's studio was filled with sketches of officers on horseback, of soldiers running, dying, or firing cannon. He had drawings of sailors tossed in a lifeboat or pulling other sailors from the water, and sketches of fortifications, gunboats and "every instrument of destruction." He was "literally laying siege to Gibraltar," one reporter wrote.

Copley changed the composition many times, but finally after two years of work he sketched the scene on canvas. Many English officers came to have their portraits painted. So impressed was General Eliott that Copley captured his likeness in just one hour that he offered to pay the artist's way to Germany in order to paint portraits of the other officers.

In August, 1787, Copley, Sukey, and Elizabeth arrived in Flanders. The ride through gentle green country to Germany helped Sukey forget the tragic days at George Street. Copley stopped in the cities long enough to study Rubens' paintings, marveling at the great master's glowing colors and energetic compositions.

He did not linger long in Germany. In a few days he painted brilliant portraits of four German officers who had fought in the siege of Gibraltar. A few weeks later the Copleys returned refreshed to George Street. Copley climbed onto the platform in his studio and brushed in the heads of the German officers, but the enormous canvas was still unfinished. The city council waited two more years.

In the spring of 1791, eight years after Copley had begun the painting, "The Siege of Gibraltar" was ready to be shown.

COLONEL ERNST AUGUST VON HUGO and
LIEUT. COLONEL VON SCHLEPPENGULL.
Study for THE SIEGE OF GIBRALTAR

1787. (26″ × 22″)

Fogg Art Museum, Harvard University, Cambridge, Mass.

Gift of Mrs. Gordon Dexter

One day in April, 1791, an enormous tent was set up in Green Park. Nearby residents protested violently, complaining that Copley's pavilion blocked their view and that the noise of visitors would disturb their peace. Several times Copley was forced to move his tent, and each time residents complained. For two months Londoners waited impatiently to see "The Siege of Gibraltar." Finally King George sent word that Copley could place his pavilion near the palace.

"My wife won't complain," the genial king remarked.

King George, the queen, and the princesses were the first visitors to the tent. During the summer thousands of people came to see "The Siege of Gibraltar." Many praised the portrait heads, but few were enthusiastic about the crowded composition. When the exhibit closed Copley asked the city council for more money. He reminded the committee that the picture had taken eight years to paint, that the tent had cost fifteen thousand dollars, and that the engravings of the painting were still unfinished. The committee turned him down.

Copley began to worry.

"May God . . . cause you to succeed in all your undertakings," his mother had written him three years before. Now his mother was dead, and his Boston farm had been sold at far too low a price. When he appealed to his Boston agent he was told that a British resident could not claim property in America. Young John Copley, now a brilliant law student, offered to plead his father's case. In 1796 he sailed for Boston. He wrote enthusiastic letters to Elizabeth about the vigorous country where he was born. He loved the pretty girls, the sleigh rides, and the clear cold climate; but, he wrote, "My father I fear is disappointed," for he could not claim the Boston farm. Perhaps Copley would consider moving to America.

"The state of society and government would be more congenial to your inclinations," he wrote his father. A few weeks later John returned to London.

Copley thought longingly about his farm on Beacon Hill, but how could he take Sukey and the children away from London where they felt so much at home? In spite of his money worries he was now well known in England and was receiving more commissions than he had time to fill.

THE SIEGE OF GIBRALTAR
1783–91. (214″ × 297″)
Guildhall Art Gallery, London

Each year Copley became more unpopular at the Academy. Members scowled when the crusty artist rose to speak against every proposal made by the new president, Benjamin West. From time to time he would exhibit a few portraits at the Academy, but he continued to show his big historical paintings in a tent.

Some of Copley's canvases pictured events which had happened many years before and others recorded recent history. Each represented years of conscientious work. Sometimes he traveled miles to paint portraits for these pictures. Elizabeth often accompanied her father on his trips and read to him while he painted.

In 1800, the excursions with his favorite daughter ended. In July, Elizabeth was married to prosperous Gardiner Greene from Boston. Copley took time to sketch a portrait of his beloved daughter before she sailed for America with her husband.

Copley had little time to write, but Sukey, John, and Mary sent Elizabeth news of George Street. Copley was visiting Sir Edward Knatchbull in his "spacious and splendid mansion," wrote young John Copley, "rain and thunder, eating and drinking, talking and laughing—such is a rough sketch of my father's first vist," he continued.

"Your father returned . . . in very good health and spirits," wrote Sukey three months later; "he has the picture of the Knatchbull family much advanced." The big canvas showed the widower in hunting costume with his ten children.

"The whole family is uncommonly handsome," continued Sukey. The next year she wrote that Sir Edward had remarried and "Must now have his present lady" and their baby added. After Copley had changed the composition, Sir Edward decided that the picture should include his two former wives.

In the spring of 1803, Sukey wrote that "the family picture" was at last completed; "we hope it will go to the exhibiton," she wrote, but Sir Edward's wife refused to have it shown because the two former wives looked like angels suspended in the sky.

The picture stayed in Copley's studio for four years, until he painted out the angels and sent the canvas back to Knatchbull.

Sketch for THE KNATCHBULL FAMILY

1800–02. (25½″ × 37½″)

Collection Lord Brabourne, Mersham Le Hatch, Kent, England

"Your father is . . . as usual painting . . . not wanting to be disturbed by the din of war," wrote Sukey in 1803. The threat of invasion by Napoleon did not worry Copley as much as his troubles with his engravers. The prints of Gibraltar were still unfinished and Copley feared that he could not afford to keep the house on George Street.

"I thought I had provided for these," he wrote to Gardiner Greene in Boston, "but I have been unjustly deprived." Apologetically he asked his son-in-law to lend him money.

Two years later Copley wrote again to Boston. The war was bad for the sale of paintings, he explained, and the engravings of "Gibraltar" were still unfinished.

Sometimes he wondered if he was too old to paint. At sixty-five he found he worked more slowly. His legs ached and his painting hand grew numb, but he continued to work on a big portrait of the Prince of Wales on horseback.

"His Royal Highness . . . shows himself much interested in the picture; he is to sit for the likeness when he returns to town," wrote Sukey to her daughter.

Copley waited three years for the prince to pose.

"It is impossible to describe . . . the perseverance of your father," wrote Sukey, when Copley sent the finished picture to the Academy. "But," she continued, "we must be prepared for criticism." The critics judged the picture harshly. The bright colors were offensive and the figures in the background looked as if they were made of tin.

That fall Copley faced another disappointment. When the "Gibraltar" engravings were finally printed, most of the subscribers, tired of waiting, cancelled their subscriptions. Again Copley had to ask Mr. Greene to send him money.

In the summer of 1815 Sukey wrote happily about peace in Europe. The "mighty conqueror" Napoleon had been defeated, but the news from George Street was less good.

"Your father grows feeble in his limbs," she wrote, although he was still painting portraits in his studio.

Then on September 9th, Mary wrote her sister that "our beloved father is no more." She was grateful that his final illness had not been long.

"He was perfectly resigned and willing to die," she assured her sister, "and expressed his firm trust in God."

GEORGE IV (As Prince of Wales)
1804–10. (147½″ × 125½″)

Courtesy, Museum of Fine Arts, Boston, Mass.

Bequest of Susan Greene Dexter in memory of Charles and Martha Babcock Amory

BIBLIOGRAPHY

Amory, Martha Babcock. *The Domestic and Artistic Life of John Singleton Copley, R.A.* Houghton Mifflin Co., Boston: 1882.

Bayley, Frank William. *The Life and Works of John Singleton Copley.* Founded on the work of Augustus Thorndike Perkins. The Taylor Press, Boston: 1915.

Coatsworth, Elizabeth. *Boston Bells.* The Macmillan Co., New York: 1952.

Copley, John Singleton. *Letters and Papers of John Singleton Copley and Henry Pelham. 1739–1776.* The Massachusetts Historical Society, Boston: 1914.

Flexner, James Thomas. *First Flowers of Our Wilderness.* Houghton Mifflin Co., Boston: 1947.

————*John Singleton Copley.* Houghton Mifflin Co., Boston: 1948.

Hagen, Oskar. *The Birth of the American Tradition in Art.* Charles Scribner's Sons, New York: 1940.

Lee, Cuthbert. *Early American Portrait Painters,* Yale University Press, New Haven: 1929.

McSpadden, J. Walker. *Famous Painters of America.* Dodd, Mead and Co., New York: 1923.

New York, Metropolitan Museum of Art. *An Exhibition of Paintings by John Singleton Copley.* December 22, 1936 to February 14, 1937.

Ollier, Edmund. *Our British Portrait Painters.* J. B. Lippincott Co., Philadelphia: 1873.

Parker, Mrs. Barbara Neville. *John Singleton Copley.* American Portraits in Oil, Pastel, and Miniature with Biographical Sketches by Barbara Neville Parker and Anne Bolling Wheeler. Museum of Fine Arts, Boston: 1938.

Prown, David Jules. *John Singleton Copley.* Two volumes. Harvard University Press, Cambridge: 1966.

U.S. National Gallery of Art. *John Singleton Copley. 1738–1815.* Catalogue of an Exhibition held at the National Gallery of Art, Washington, D.C., the Metropolitan Museum of Art, New York, Museum of Fine Arts, Boston. 1965–66.

Whitely, William T. *Artists and Their Friends in England. 1700–1799.* Two volumes. The Medici Society, London and Boston: 1928.

INDEX